Affirmations

Affirmations

*Joyful and Creative
Exuberance*

Paul Kurtz

 Prometheus Books
59 John Glenn Drive
Amherst, New York 14228-2197

Published 2004 by Prometheus Books

Inquiries should be addressed to
Prometheus Books
59 John Glenn Drive
Amherst, New York 14228–2197
VOICE: 716–691–0133, ext. 207
FAX: 716–564–2711
WWW.PROMETHEUSBOOKS.COM

11 10 09 08 07   11 10 9 8 7 6

Library of Congress Cataloging-in-Publication Data

Kurtz, Paul, 1925–
    Affirmations : joyful and creative exuberance / by Paul Kurtz.
        p. cm.
    ISBN 13: 978-1-59102-389-0
    ISBN 10: 1-59102-389-0 (pbk. : alk. paper)

    1. Humanism. I. Title.

BL2747.6.K85 2004
171'.2--dc22

                                                    2004007393

Printed in the United States on acid-free paper

Contents

Contents

Prefatory

*T*his little book is made up of a series of affirmations of humanist *eupraxsophy*, which means good, practical wisdom. They present ideas that are naturalistic and secular, a new Humanist testament, as it were.

Some were gleaned from my earlier writings. Some are revised and rewritten. Others are entirely new.

I offer them to the reader with loving care and affection, in the hope that they can provide guidelines for courageous inquirers seeking paths toward a New Enlightenment.

Although based on scientific rationality and moral reflection, they are, I trust, infused with feeling and compassion for the human condition and our shared planetary habitat. They express the conviction that every person has some measure of power for achieving joyful and creative exuberance.

—Paul Kurtz

One

The
Affirmations
of
Humanism

*H*umanists are committed to the application of reason and science to the understanding of the universe and to the solving of human problems.

* We want to protect and enhance the Earth, to preserve it for future generations, and to avoid inflicting needless suffering on other species.

* We attempt to transcend divisive parochial loyalties based on race, religion, gender, nationality, creed, class, sexual orientation, or ethnicity, and strive to work together for the common good of humanity.

* We believe in an open and pluralistic society, and that democracy is the best guarantee of protecting human rights from authoritarian elites and repressive majorities.

* We believe in the cultivation of moral excellence.

* We believe in the common moral decencies: altruism, integrity, honesty, truthfulness, fairness, responsibility. Humanist ethics is amenable to critical, rational guidance. There are normative standards that we discover together. Moral principles are tested by their consequences.

* We are deeply concerned with the moral education of our children. We want to nourish reason and compassion.

* We believe that scientific discovery and technology can contribute to the betterment of human life.

* We cultivate the arts of negotiation and compromise as a means of resolving differences and achieving mutual understanding.

* We are concerned with securing justice and fairness in society and with eliminating discrimination and intolerance.

* We are committed to the principle of the separation of church and state.

* We believe in supporting the disadvantaged and the handicapped so that they will be able to help themselves.

* We believe in enjoying life here and now and in developing our creative talents to their fullest.

* We respect the right to privacy. Mature adults should be allowed to fulfill their aspirations, to express their sexual preferences, to exercise reproductive freedom, to have access to comprehensive and informed healthcare, and to die with dignity.

* We are engaged by the arts no less than by the sciences.

* We are citizens of the universe and are excited by the prospect of discoveries still to be made in the cosmos.

* We are skeptical of untested claims to knowledge, and we are open to novel ideas and seek new departures in our thinking.

* We affirm humanism as a realistic alternative to theologies of despair and ide-

ologies of violence and as a source of rich personal significance and genuine satisfaction in the service to others.

* We believe in optimism rather than pessimism, hope rather than despair, learning in the place of dogma, truth instead of ignorance, joy rather than guilt or sin, tolerance in the place of fear, love instead of hatred, compassion over selfishness, beauty instead of ugliness, and reason rather than blind faith or irrationality.

* We believe in the fullest realization of the best and noblest that we are capable of as human beings.

Two

The New Skepticism

*T*he methods of critical inquiry used so
effectively in science need to be extended to
all areas of human interest. Beliefs should be
treated as hypotheses and be tested by evidence, logical coherence, and experimental
consequences. All claims to knowledge should
be open to revision in the light of inquiry. As
a result, there is a progressive growth of
knowledge.

Skeptical inquiry is essential for the development of human knowledge. It represents a historic tradition in science, philosophy, and learning. We may distinguish skeptical inquiry, with emphasis on *inquiry*, from classical skepticism, which was apt to be totally negative, even nihilistic. This form of skepticism is a *new skepticism*, for it is positive and constructive; its principles are essential for the development of knowledge about nature and human behavior. Moreover, its methods are relevant to the solution of ethical, political, and social problems.

With these considerations in mind, a set of principles serves as guidelines for skeptical inquirers:

* ✳ We believe in the possibility of discovering reliable human knowledge. We affirm the positive powers of human intelligence. We believe that the methods of scientific inquiry can expand the frontiers of knowledge and that these can be used for the betterment of humankind.

* We submit that skepticism is an essential part of *scientific inquiry* and that it should be extended to all areas of human endeavor, science, everyday life, law, religion and the paranormal, economics, politics, ethics, and society—and that the standards of rationality apply to each area of human interest.

* We believe that critical thinking is inherent in all worthwhile inquiry about the world, and that it can be enlisted to solve problems, neutralize animosities, compromise hatred, and negotiate differences.

* We believe in clarity rather than obfuscation, lucidity in the place of confusion, linguistic definitions to overcome vagueness or ambiguity.

* We do not reject any claim to knowledge prior to inquiry. We insist, however, that claims be framed in testable form and that the burden of proof rests

primarily with the party asserting the claim.

✱ We ask for facts, not suppositions; experimental evidence, not anecdotal hearsay or conjecture; logical inference and deduction, not faith or intuition.

✱ We do not believe in absolute dogmas or creeds, whether set in stone or proclaimed as official doctrine.

✱ We reject mythologies of salvation, old or new, whether based in ancient fears or current messianic illusions, unsubstantiated by corroborative empirical grounds. We believe in inquiry rather than authority, reason in the place of tradition.

✱ We maintain that reason and science can be used to develop new technologies, alleviate suffering and reduce pain, ameliorate and enhance human happiness.

✳ We submit that rational inquiry can
help us to develop and test ethical
principles, moral values, and social
policies, and thus can contribute to
human well-being.

✳ We are not negative skeptics, naysayers,
debunkers, cynics, or nihilists. We simply
wish to oppose hypocrisy and cant,
deception, and illusion. We emphasize
instead the tests of evidence and rationality. In short, we believe that critical
inquiry is the best way to framing our
means and fulfilling our ends.

Three

A New Paradigm

A new paradigm is emerging today:

* It is committed to *free inquiry* in all areas of human interest.

* It believes that reliable knowledge is possible. It considers beliefs as hypotheses to be tested by their experimental consequences and rational consistency.

* It is *naturalistic*. It wishes to extend the methods of science and reason to understanding nature and solving human problems.

* It is *skeptical*. It doubts claims for which insufficient evidence or reasons exist, including claims of revelation, mysticism, faith, authority, or tradition.

* It emphasizes *education*, the cultivation of *critical thinking*, and reasoned *persuasion* as the best means of achieving social change.

* It is thoroughly *humanistic*.

* It concentrates on ways of realizing and embracing human happiness in this world.

* It seeks common ground with other human beings: universal rights, shared interests, and common values. It is tolerant of different lifestyles.

✳ It wishes to maximize the values of *creativity* and *self-realization*.

✳ It is concerned with the *secular city*. It seeks to separate the state from the church (or mosque or temple), politics from theology, and civic morality from religion.

✳ It is *democratic*. It emphasizes the dignity and worth of every person; it seeks to extend the dimensions of human freedom; it believes in social justice, equality, and fairness; it wishes to afford each individual the opportunity to achieve the good life.

✳ It strives to rise above the narrow parochial interests of the past in order to build a *global community* based on planetary ethics.

✳ It is *optimistic*, though *realistic*, in that it has confidence in the ability of humans to solve their problems.

* It cultivates *goodwill*. It prefers the *arts of negotiation*, compromise, and the peaceful resolution of conflicts to violence or force.

* It is *melioristic*, believing that it is possible to create a better world.

* It does not counsel retreat into a mood of passive acceptance or piety, but wishes to actuate the virtue of *courage*, the fortitude to overcome and achieve what we believe in.

* It focuses not on the tragic dimensions of human existence, angst, or despair, but on the quest for the best that we are capable of achieving—in human terms, the *bountiful life* of *excellence and nobility* for ourselves and other human beings.

* It aims to develop human *wisdom* as a guide to life.

Four

Eupraxsophy

*T*here is no word in the English language
that adequately conveys the meaning of
humanism. It is *not* a religion; it represents a
philosophical, scientific, and ethical outlook. I
have accordingly introduced a new term—
eupraxsophy—in order to distinguish humanistic convictions and practices from religious
systems of faith and belief.

This term can be used in many languages.
It is derived from Greek roots: *eu-*, *praxis*,
and *sophia*.

Eu- is a prefix that means "good," "well," "advantageous." It is found in the Greek word *eudaimonia*, which means "well-being" or "happiness," and it is also used in terms such as *eulogy* and *euphoria*.

Praxis (or *prassein*) refers to "action, doing, or practice." *Eupraxia* means "right action" or "good conduct."

Sophia means "wisdom." This word appears in *philosophy*, combining *philo-* ("loving") and *sophia* ("wisdom") to mean "love of wisdom."

Eupraxsophy is designed for the public arena where ideas contend. Unlike pure philosophy, it focuses not simply on the *love* of wisdom, though this is surely implied by it, but the *practice* of wisdom. Moral philosophers should be interested in developing the capacity for critical ethical judgments. That is an eminent goal. But eupraxsophy goes further than that, for it focuses on creating a coherent ethical life stance. Moreover, it presents hypotheses and theories about nature and the cosmos that at any particular point in history are based on the best scientific knowledge of the day. Humanist eupraxsophy defends a set of criteria evaluating the testing of truth claims. It may espouse at any one time in history a particular set of political ideals. Eupraxsophy combines both a Weltanschauung and a philosophy of living. But it takes us one step further by means of commitment; based upon cognition, it is fused with passion. It entails the application of wisdom to the conduct of life.

Eupraxsophers make choices—the most reasonable ones in the light of the best available evidence—and this enables them to act. Theologians, politicians, generals, engineers, businessmen, lawyers, doctors, artists, poets, and plain men and women have beliefs upon which they act. Why deny this right to the informed eupraxsopher-scientist-philosopher? It is our conviction, however, that one's beliefs should be based upon reason, critical intelligence, and wisdom. This is what the suffix *sophy* refers to. Wisdom in the broad sense includes not only philosophical and practical judgments, but scientific understanding.

Intrinsic to this definition is a scientific

component, for wisdom includes the most reliable knowledge drawn from scientific research and scholarship in the various fields of inquiry. Theoretical research is morally neutral. The scientist is interested in developing causal hypotheses and theories that can be verified by the evidence. Scientists describe or explain how the subject under study behaves, without evaluating it normatively.

Humanist eupraxsophy, on the other hand, attempts to draw the philosophical implications of the sciences to the lives of men and women. It seeks to develop a cosmic perspective which is based on the most reliable findings discovered on the frontiers of science. It recognizes that there are gaps in our current knowledge that still need to be investigated. It is keenly aware of human fallibility about what we do and do not know, yet it boldly applies practical scientific wisdom to life.

Accordingly, the primary task of eupraxsophy is to understand nature and life and to draw concrete normative prescriptions from this knowledge. Eupraxsophy involves a double focus: a cosmic perspective and a set of normative principles and values by which we may live.

Humanists do not look upward to a heaven for a promise of divine deliverance. They have their feet planted squarely in nature, yet they have the fortitude to employ art, science, reason, sympathy, and education to create a better world for themselves and their fellow human beings.

From the standpoint of the individual, happiness is achieved not by a passive release from the world, but by the pursuit of an active life of adventure and fulfillment. There are so many opportunities for creative enjoyment that every moment can be viewed as precious; all fit together to make a full and exuberant life.

What is vital in humanist eupraxsophy is that humanists are not overwhelmed by the tragic character of the human condition; they are willing to face death, sorrow, adversity, and suffering with courage and equanimity. They have confidence in the ability of human beings to overcome alienation, solve the problems of living, and develop the capacity to share the material goods of life with others and empathize with them. The theist often has a degraded view of human beings, who, beset with original sin, are incapable of solving life's problems by themselves and need to look outside of the human realm for divine succor. The humanist accepts the fact that the human species has imperfections and limitations and that some things encountered in existence may be beyond redress or repair. Even so, he or she is convinced that the best posture is not to retreat before the unknown, but to exert the intelligence and fortitude to deal with life's problems. It is only by a resolute appraisal of the human condition, based on reason and science, that the humanist's life stance seems most appropriate. The secular humanist is unwilling to bow before either the forces of nature or would-be human masters. Rather, he or she expresses the highest heroic virtues of the Promethean spirit: audacity, nobility, and developed moral sensibilities about the needs of others!

Five

The Common Moral Decencies

*T*he question is often asked: Can a society or person be moral without religious faith? To which, I respond, yes, indeed; morality is deeply rooted in the "common moral decencies" as they relate to moral behavior in society.

The common moral decencies are widely shared. They are practiced by religious and nonreligious folks alike. They are essential to the survival of any community. Meaningful coexistence cannot occur if they are consistently flouted. Handed down through countless generations, they are recognized throughout history by friends and relatives, colleagues and coworkers, native-born and immigrant. They are basic normative rules of social intercourse. They provide the very foundations of moral education and are taught to the young in the family and the schools. They express the elementary virtues of courtesy, politeness, and empathy so essential for living together; indeed, they are the basis of civilized life itself.

The common moral decencies are transcultural in their range. They have their roots in generic human needs. They no doubt grow out of the long evolutionary struggle for survival and may even have sociobiological roots, though they may be lacking in some individuals or societies, since their emergence depends upon the presence of certain preconditions of moral and social development. Here is a partial list of the decencies:

* First are the moral decencies that involve *personal integrity*, that is,

telling the truth, not lying or being deceitful; being *sincere*, candid, frank, and free of hypocrisy; *keeping one's promises*, honoring pledges, living up to agreements; and *being honest*, avoiding fraud or skullduggery.

✳ Second is *trustworthiness*. We manifest *loyalty* to our loved ones, relatives, friends, and coworkers. We should be *dependable*, people who other people can count on. We should be *reliable* and responsible.

✳ Third are the decencies of *benevolence*, which involve manifesting *goodwill* and noble intentions toward other human beings and having a positive concern for them. It means the *lack of malice* (nonmalfeasance), avoiding doing harm to other persons or their property: We should not kill or rob; inflict physical violence or injury; or be cruel, abusive, or vengeful. In the sexual domain it means that we should not force our sexual passions on others and we should seek *mutual consent* between adults. It means that we have an obligation to be *beneficent*, kind, sympathetic, and compassionate. We should lend a helping hand to those in distress and, when we can, try to decrease their pain and suffering and contribute positively to their welfare.

✳ Fourth is the principle of *fairness*. We should show *gratitude* and appreciation for those who are deserving of it. A civilized community will hold people *accountable* for their deeds, insisting that those who wrong others do not escape completely or go unpunished, and perhaps they must make reparations to the aggrieved. This also involves the principles of *justice* and *equality* in society. *Tolerance* is also a basic moral decency: We should allow other individuals the right to their beliefs, values, and styles of life, even though they may differ from our own.

We may not agree with them, but each person is entitled to his or her convictions as long as he or she does not harm others or prevent them from exercising their rights. We should try to *cooperate* with others, seeking to *negotiate differences peacefully* without resorting to hatred or violence.

These common moral decencies express general principles and rules. Though individuals or nations may deviate from practicing them, they nonetheless provide parameters by which to guide conduct. Some are so cherished that we are reluctant to violate them. Nevertheless, they are not absolutes, and they may at times conflict; we may have to establish priorities among them. They need not be divinely ordained to need moral force, for they are tested in the last analysis by their *consequences* in practice and their essential centrality to life. Morally developed human beings accept these principles and attempt to live by them because they understand that some personal moral sacrifices may be necessary to avoid conflict in living and working together. Practical moral wisdom thus recognizes the obligatory nature of responsible conduct.

Six

Ethical Excellences

*T*he common moral decencies harmonize our relationships with other human beings. In addition, there are a number of humanistic values that we strive to realize in our *personal* lives. These are the ethical excellences. They are standards of ethical development, exquisite qualities of high merit and achievement. Once cultivated, they allow personal nobility to shine through and to flower. They are the excellences that fully realized persons best exemplify. These traits of character are good in themselves, yet they provide some balance in living. Here is a list of the key excellences of the enriched life.

* First is the excellence of *autonomy,* or what Ralph Waldo Emerson called self-reliance. This means a person's ability to take control of his or her own destiny, as far as one can, to accept responsibility for one's marriage or career, how he or she lives and learns, the most important values and goods that are cherished. Such a person is self-directed and self-governed. Personal autonomy is an affirmation of freedom. Some individuals find freedom a burden; they are willing to forfeit their right to self-determination to others—to parents or spouses, co-workers or employees, despots or gurus, prophets or profiteers. A free individual recognizes that he or she has only one life to live and that how a person lives is ultimately one's own

choice. This recognizes that we live
with others and share many values and
ideals, but basic to the ethics of
democracy is an appreciation for the
importance of individual choice, no
matter how idiosyncratic or unique it
may be.

＊ Second, *intelligence* and reason rate
high on the scale of values. To achieve
the good life we need to develop our
cognitive skills—not merely technical
expertise or skilled virtuosity, but good
judgment about how to make wise
choices and how to live. Many small-
minded critics demean human intelligence and denigrate the power of
human choice. They believe that we
cannot solve our problems by
depending solely on our own attitudes
and resources. They are willing to abdi-
cate their right to rational autonomy to
others. Reason may not succeed in
solving all problems—sometimes we
must choose the lesser of two evils or

the greater of two goods. Nevertheless, this is the most reliable method we have for framing moral choices and dealing with the quandaries of living.

* Third is the need for some *self-discipline* within the domain of passions and feelings. We need to satisfy our desires, emotions, and needs, but with some moderation, under the guidance of rational choice, recognizing the harmful consequences that imprudent choices may have upon ourselves and others. We can dream of inspiring plans and projects; and we can embrace them often only with heroic exertion and sacrifice; but not at the price of squandering our rational control.

* Fourth, some *self-respect* is vital to psychological balance. Self-hatred can consume the personality with self-doubt and cowardice. A person needs to develop some appreciation for who he or she is and a realistic sense of one's

own identity. The lack of self-esteem can denude a person, make one feel impotent and worthless. Some confidence that one *can* succeed is essential for the good life.

✳ Fifth, and esteemed highly on the scale of values, is *creativity*, the fountainhead of innovation and invention, the boundless spirit of novelty and discovery. This is closely related to autonomy and self-respect, for the independent person has some confidence in one's powers and dares to express his or her unique talents. The uncreative person is usually a conformist, unwilling to break new ground, timid and fearful of new departures. A creative person exudes a zest for life that overflows in adventure and exploration. Creativity perhaps best defines who and what we are as humans: we are the masters of our own destinies, the creators and makers of new worlds. We can add to the sum of bountiful joys implicit in the fullness of life, but only if we dare to do so.

* Sixth, we need to develop *high motivation*, be ever ready to seize the opportunities in life, to undertake new departures in thought, experience, and action. The motivated person finds life intrinsically interesting and exciting. Many people find life overwhelming; "it is boring," they say; or they find their jobs demeaning. They may be merely masking their lack of intensity in life or a lack of commitment to higher aspirations and deeper inspirations. They are willing to forfeit their lives to the banalities of taste and fashion, always following the in-crowd, afraid to be different, or to be true to their own private longings and unrealized potentialities.

* Seventh is an *affirmative* and *positive* attitude toward life. We need some measure of optimism that what we do

matters, that we *can* make our mark upon the world and change the future. Although we may suffer failure and defeat, we must believe that we shall overcome and succeed in the end despite adversity. And if we don't, we go on to the next challenge. The *courage to become* is the vital component of a life well lived. One does not betray his or her deepest strengths, but asserts them as part of the power and vibrancy of being human. We can and do express our potentialities, and we can and do capture opportunities that arise or that we can create.

❋ Eighth, an affirmative person is capable of *joie de vivre*, the intensity and passion of joyful experiences. This expresses the full range of human pleasures and satisfactions, the physical enjoyments of eating and drinking, making love and savoring sex, kissing and embracing, laughing and singing, doing good deeds for others, learning from reading and inquiring, tasting life to the fullest.

* Ninth, if we are to live well, we should be concerned about *good health* as a precondition of everything else. To achieve and maintain health we should avoid noxious drugs. We may choose to imbibe, but only in moderation. Some stress is unavoidable in life, but it should be kept within limits. We need proper nutrition, balanced diets, vigorous exercise, and sufficient rest and leisure. We need to love others and be loved by them, to share our everyday lives with friends and companions; to belong to significant communities of interaction and inquiry, work, and play; and we need times for solitude and quiet reflection.

* Tenth, all these excellences clearly point to the goodness of life. The intrinsic value we seek to achieve is creative happiness and lusty well-being.

The best word to describe such a state of living is *exuberance* or *excelsior*; it is an active life, not a total passive withdrawal. It quickens the perfection of our talents and powers, needs and wants, goals and aspirations. The end, purpose, and goal of life is to live fully and creatively, making each moment of beauty and brilliance count. The meaning of life is not to be discovered only after death in some hidden, mysterious realm, by salvation or release. That folktale has squandered countless lives in false illusions. On the contrary, the relevance of life can be found only by eating and tasting the succulent fruit of the Tree of Life and by living in the here and now with intensity and equanimity, with both rational reflection and throbbing vitality. Every moment of life is precious, intrinsically good in itself and for its own sake. The pains and sorrows, tragedies and defeats that people suffer can be outmatched by the excellences and joys,

the virtues and enrichments, the quali-
tative immediacies and adornments of
life that they can discover and *savor*.
Ah! to live and live well, to breathe and
exalt, yes, that makes it all worthwhile;
it is its own reward, the consummate
joy of being alive!

Seven

Joyful Exuberance

The Fullness of Life

*H*umanists find exuberance to be intrinsically worthwhile for its own sake. This is usually identified with happiness. The Greeks called it *eudaimonia*, or well-being: this meant the actualization of a person's nature, with pleasure as a by-product, not for the solitary moment, but in a complete life. This entails some moderation of a person's desires. But I add that in joyful exuberance there is high excitement, the intensity of living, throbbing with passion, engaging in daring activities of enterprise and adventure.

* Joyful exuberance is enhanced when we not only fulfill our needs and wants, but creatively express our goals and aspirations. It denotes some degree of excellence, nobility, even perfectibility, of a person's talents and achievements. It comes to fruition for those who find life intensely worth living and at times exhilarating.

* More than that, it involves a flowering of the personality in his or her own terms. And in its highest reaches it expresses the fullness and richness of living.

* This occurs when a person is able to realize his wants and talents, dreams and aspirations, and when a person is able to share the bountiful goods of life with others—children and parents, brothers and sisters, relatives and

friends, colleagues and neighbors—
within the various communities of
humankind. This is most eloquently
achieved when there is moral growth
and development: a person is able to
appreciate the needs of others; there is
a genuine willingness to relate to them,
to love and be loved, to share and even
to make sacrifices for their benefit.

✳ Joyful immediacies are experienced
when there is a flowering of life.
There are three *e*-words that describe
this state: *excellence, eudaimonia,* and
exuberance.

✳ And there are five *c*-words that define
it: *character, cognition, courage, creativity,* and *caring.*

✳ This does not deny or ignore the pain
and despair, defeat and failure, evil and
tragedy that may befall a person, the
unexpected contingencies of fate and for-
tune: intractable illness, premature death,

betrayal, cowardice, dishonesty, or ingratitude that may be encountered.

* The mature person has developed a reflective attitude that enables him or her to place these misadventures and setbacks, painful as they may be, in a broader context. He can compensate for the shortcomings of life by pointing to the times that he had overcome adversity; and he still finds life worth living: poetry and profundity, laughter and delight, romance and love, discovery and ingenuity, enlightenment and success, the times that he persevered and prevailed. If a person's career and life is like a work of art, then we need to appreciate its full collage, its contrasts and highlights, tones and shades, colors and forms. Marshaling some stoicism in periods of anxiety, hopefully a person will find that the good that one experiences can outbalance the bad, the positive the negative, and that optimism can master pessimism.

✳ The affirmative person may sum up his
or her life and declare that, after all is
said and done, it was worth living, that
though he may have some regrets for
what he could have done and did not, or
for what might have been but was not,
all told it was good. And, ah yes!
although there were periods of pain and
sorrow, these were balanced by those of
pleasure and joy. What an adventure it
has been—far better to have lived and
experienced, than not to have lived at all!

Eight

Eight

Creating Your Own Meanings

*T*he meaning of life is not to be found in a secret formula discovered by ancient prophets or modern gurus, who withdraw from living to seek quiet contemplation and release. Life has no meaning per se; it does, however, present us with innumerable opportunities, which we can either squander and retreat from in fear or seize with exuberance.

✳ It can be discovered by anyone and everyone who can energize an inborn zest for living. It is found within living itself, as it reaches out to create new conditions for experience.

✳ Eating of the fruit of the Tree of Life gives us the bountiful enthusiasms for living. The ultimate value is the conviction that life can be found good in and of itself. Each moment has a kind of preciousness and attractiveness.

✳ The so-called secret of life is an open scenario that can be deciphered by everyone. It is found in the experiences of living: in the delights of a fine banquet, the strenuous exertion of hard work, the poignant melodies of a symphony, the appreciation of an altruistic deed, the excitement of an embrace of someone you love, the elegance of a mathematical proof, the invigorating adventure of a mountain climb, the satisfaction of quiet relaxation, the lusty

singing of an anthem, the vigorous
cheering in a sports contest, the
reading of a delicate sonnet, the joys of
parenthood, the pleasures of friendship,
the quiet gratification of serving our
fellow human beings—in all of these
activities and more.

* It is in the present moment of experience as it is brought to fruition, as well
as in the delicious memory of past
experiences and the expectation of
future ones, that the richness of life is
exemplified and realized. The meaning
of life is that it can be found to be
good and beautiful and exciting on its
own terms for ourselves, our loved
ones, and other sentient beings. It is
found in the satisfaction intrinsic to
creative activities, wisdom, and right-
eousness. One doesn't need more than
that and hopefully one will not settle
for less.

* The meaning of life is tied up intimately with our plans and projects, the goals we set for ourselves, our dreams, and the successful achievement of them.

* We create our own conscious meanings; we invest the cultural and natural worlds with our own interpretations. We discover, impose upon, and add to nature.

* Meaning is found in the lives of the ancient Egyptians, in their culture built around Isis and Osiris and the pyramids, or in the ruminations of the ancient prophets of the Old Testament. It is exemplified by the Athenian philosopher standing in the Acropolis deliberating about justice in the city-state. It is seen in the structure of the medieval town, built upon a rural economy, feudalism, and a Christian cultural backdrop. It is experienced by the Samurai warrior in the context of

Japanese culture, in the hopes and dreams of the Incas of Peru, by the native Watusi tribes in Africa, and in the Hindu and Muslim cultures of India and southern Asia. And it is exemplified anew in modern postindustrial technological urban civilizations of the present-day world, which give us new cultural materials and new opportunities for adventure.

✱ Human beings have found their meanings within the context of a historical cultural experience, and in how they are able to live and participate within it. Life had meaning to them; only the content differed; the form and function were similar. Life, when fully lived under a variety of cultural conditions, can be euphoric and optimistic; it can be a joy to experience and a wonder to behold.

Nine

Eroticism

* A vital ingredient of the full life is the
  ability to enjoy pleasures that are
  erotic, to find delight in the sensual, to
  be aroused by beauty, to be allured by
  the caress of touch, to savor the sensuous form and the fragrance and
  romance of sexuality and love.

* Although the good life involves the
  active mood, the strenuous attitude of
  exertion and achievement, it also

involves some rest and repose, the ability to capture moments of tender feeling and enraptured ecstasy.

✳ Not to suffer the lures and pangs of passion, or to be moved by its fervor and attraction, is not to have lived fully; without passion, life would be lacking something poignant. The erotic thus plays a significant role in the full life.

✳ Yet, there are the disciples of "virtue" and the crusaders against "sin" who consider the main problems in life to be the extirpation or control of the erotic. *Erotic-phobia* is only one aspect of a broader *hedonic-phobia*, or distaste for pleasure. Those who oppose the erotic are the enemies of human life.

✳ Eroticism has many dimensions. It arouses within us an appreciation for love. *Eros*, son of Aphrodite, was the god of love; and the *erotic* is related to romantic affection. But it also focuses on the pleasures of sexual arousal that culminates in orgasm. Beginning with sexual intercourse, it leads to an appreciation of a wide range of sexual tastes and passions—from the kiss and touch to fondling, caressing, and other forms of erotic stimulation.

* The erotic can be diffused; it can assume a variety of expressions. Having its roots in sexual acts, it may be elaborated with subtlety and delicacy. Being open to the erotic is to enter a new world of *aesthetic-hedonic* appreciation: the capacity for discovering the pleasures of the sensuous as they are revealed in ourselves and others. To be closed to those pleasures is to be blind to the full richness of life.

Ten

Loving Another Person

* The sharing of life with another human being can be an eloquent and profound source of affection.

* A person can relate to another person on many levels—not only through sexual passion, but also through altruistic love, the joining together of careers, raising children, living together, sharing a home, and pursuing activities cooperatively.

❋ To lead a solitary life and to do things by and for oneself is fairly common; some individuals say they do not wish to enter into relationships they consider confining. Yet to be denied love for those who crave it but cannot be fulfilled breeds desperation.

❋ Many have discovered that to partake of life with another person can be the well-spring of the deepest human fulfillment.

❋ If a person has someone to love romantically—and that love is requited— he or she can remove the outer mask worn in the public places of commerce, and he or she can experience the private joys and sorrows of life with another without the need for pretense.

❋ Accordingly, the opportunity to share life intimately with another human being is a priceless adornment of a life

well lived, a thing of beauty intrinsically worthwhile in itself.

Eleven

A
Good Marriage
or
Civil Union

* A good marriage or civil union is one where each partner discovers that it is better to give love than to receive it.

* To truly love another person is to wish that person to develop and flourish on his or her own terms.

* In an enduring marriage or partnership there will be joy and laughter, but also sadness and sorrow, harmony and dis-

cord, as each strives to overcome adversity and to fulfill private dreams and shared aspirations.

✳ The key value of a viable union is that it allows for intimacy between two persons who can enjoy each other's company, prize common ideals and expectations, confess failures and admit defeats, and yet realize the qualities of the good life together.

✳ As a couple builds a home, embarks upon careers, and perhaps raises a family, the marriage can become a work of art in which both partners give it line and form, color and tone.

✳ Individuals who are married will be challenged every day and in every way to make their relationship work. If they do, it can become a cherished creation of aesthetic splendor and enduring value.

Twelve

Being a Loving Parent

* Genuinely loving parents will do their best for their children, but this includes the willingness to allow their children to become persons. Let the child become whatever he or she wishes. We provide guidance and sustenance where it is needed, and indeed make continuing sacrifices for

their well-being, but if we love our
children, we want them to develop
their own unique personalities.

* We can love our children even though
  we may disagree fundamentally with
  their choice of a mate, career, or
  lifestyle.

* We should make allowances for our
  children, recognize their limitations as
  well as their virtues, not demand the
  impossible, but love them for what
  they are.

* We ought to nourish and cultivate our
  children's physical and mental growth.
  At some point we should be prepared
  to let young persons go out into the
  world, to discover and create their own
  destiny.

* To love someone in a healthy sense—
  whether a husband or wife, a son or
  daughter—is to want that person to

flourish in his or her own terms and to develop some autonomy. Parents should not give unconditionally to their children and never expect anything in return. Such a relationship would be debilitating to both the child and the parent.

* Loving parents should try to develop creativity in their children, to cultivate their individuality, assertiveness, independence, and freedom. But they also need to nourish in them their responsibilities to others.

* Loving parents want their children to be persons of integrity and honor. If they do not demonstrate to them the importance of giving love as well as receiving it, then they have indeed failed.

* To love our children for their sake is its own reward. To have them return that love and affection to us—and others—

is the eloquent bond that enables
moral growth to blossom.

Thirteen

The Beloved Cause

❋ To be loyal to a cause that outreaches a person's own parochial interests is to widen the range of one's horizons as a person. Too many individuals are overly concerned with their day-to-day cares of making a living and fulfilling their limited goals; as such, they may be overly focused on a narrow circle of friends and interests. To take the larger perceptive can be a source of enlightenment and freedom; it can emancipate us from bondage to trivia.

＊ One can share with others a dedication to a greater dream. One can live, in part, for a noble cause. There are any number of causes that we can strive for. They are as multifarious and diverse as culture itself: feeding the hungry; housing the homeless; working for peace, democracy, or world government; campaigning for a political party or candidate; working for freedom or justice or equal rights; spreading learning and enlightenment throughout the world; joining the conservationist movement or propagating the faith to stamp out cancer, fascism, or alcoholism.

＊ Espousing and working for a cause— whatever it is—is important for the person so involved, for it enables him or her to transcend his restricted circle.

✳ To be interested in the cause of others and to wish to share enthusiasm with them is to contribute to one's growth as a person.

✳ One's private aims are surely worthy of effort and energy, but broader aims may equally have a claim upon one's energy and devotion.

✳ To be indifferent to the needs of our time and to the broader movements of social change is to be morally insensitive.

✳ We need to cultivate some fervor and commitment to the beloved vision of a better world; and *loyalty to loyalty* is itself a moral value.

Fourteen

Planetary Humanism

*T*he optimum way of solving political and social questions is to rely on "the method of intelligence." Though the content of our political programs and policies may vary, the methodology of critical intelligence is the most reliable guide for social action.

There are three general moral principles on the sociopolitical level to which we are devoted:

✳ First is the commitment to *democracy*.
An educated citizenry is the best guarantee of achieving the public good.
The democratic society depends on an
open society, civil liberties, a free press,
majority rule and minority rights, the
legal right of opposition, and due
process of law. A free market of ideas is
an essential condition for ensuring
both human liberty and equal rights.

✳ Second is the importance of *secularism*,
the separation of state and church and
opposition to any effort to impose a
religious test for public office. Theo-
cratic powers should not be permitted
to dictate public policies.

✳ A third vital principle has emerged
today on the planetary scale: we have
an obligation to our habitat, the planet
Earth, and the world community.
Accordingly, the ethics of humanism
applies to the entire human family on
the planetary level. Spurred on by the

adventures of space exploration, it is grounded in the recognition of our global interdependence. Our moral responsibilities do not end at the perimeters of our own locality, region, or nation, but encompass the entire globe. Our moral obligations apply to *all* members of the planetary community, not only the human ones.

Implicit in Planetary Humanism are the following imperatives:

* Our actions should be judged by their effects on those we encounter in our communities of interaction. This must be extended to the larger planetary focus: the blue-green dot as viewed from outer space.

* We ought not to pollute, destroy, or degrade the natural ecology.

* We ought to be concerned with the well-being and happiness of *all mem-*

bers of the human species on the planet,
each of whom ought to be considered as
equal in dignity and value.

These imperatives are apparent when we
observe

* the callous misuse of common global
  resources

* the uncontrolled growth of populations

* the degradation of our planetary envi-
  ronment

* the increase in global warming

* the disparities in wealth and income

* the rise of self-righteous fanaticism and
  terrorism

* the constant resort to violence and war
  to resolve differences.

Given these problems a new ethical commitment has emerged: *We each have obligations both to present and future generations, and to the preservation, enhancement, and well-being of all life on the planet Earth.*

Fifteen

Aphorisms of the Good Will

*T*here are a number of matrix aphorisms and maxims of the good will that we can catalogue. We should:

* Express an affirmative attitude toward others and ourselves.

* Compliment people if they do well; be polite, honest, and considerate.

* Try to find the best in individuals, not their faults or shortcomings.

* Applaud people's achievements, appreciate their creativity, respect their uniqueness.

* Learn to forgive and forget, to heal and respect, to modify and improve.

* Do not return evil for evil; do not be vengeful, vindictive, or spiteful.

* Learn to make exceptions, be flexible.

* Be willing to change your mind and to admit when you are wrong.

* Try to help others if you can; be pleased if they succeed.

* Abandon jealousy, hatred, cynicism, revenge, or greed.

* Enjoy life, lessen your complaints, point out its beauty or value, not its imperfections.

* Instead of bemoaning your fate or blaming others, pitch in and try to improve the situation.

* Seek to better the human condition, be constructive.

* Recognize that no one is perfect.

* Accept people for what they are, including their idiosyncrasies.

* Give people some latitude to succeed and achieve, and they will.

* Respect innovation, individuality, creativity, honest dissent.

* Have the courage of your convictions; do not be afraid to express them.

* Always try to exude a cheerful, optimistic, affirmative attitude, especially where conditions warrant it.

* Focus on potential good, not possible evil, honor not betrayal, collegiality not hatred, justice not injustice.

* Hold people accountable if they have been immoral; protect those they harm; ask for reparations if they are due; be merciful, and understanding.

* Compromise differences, negotiate solutions.

* Avoid violence or force and seek a peaceful resolution of differences.

* Try to find common ground, shared moral principles, and values upon which we can stand and unite.

A GOOD WILL

* It is an eloquent expression of the exuberant life.

* It bestows benefits on both the giver and receiver.

* It is an expression of human caring.

* It is a precious quality of a life well-lived.

WHY

The question is raised, "Why?": to which I respond, because these, as set forth, are the transformational matrix principles of civilized conduct, because in expressing a good will you not only add to the sum of human happiness, but do the right thing. Indeed, of all human qualities and possessions, a good will is the most cherished.

Sixteen

Facing Death with Courage

* The ultimate good for each person and the basic source of all human value is life. There is a constant struggle of living things to thwart death, to stave it off, to keep living and functioning at all costs. Yet perhaps the only certainty in an otherwise ambiguous universe is that one's life will someday cease.

* At some point every person will have to come to terms with death. Indeed,

life may not have meaning in a full sense unless and until we face death. It is only out of that existential confrontation that things can be placed in their proper perspective and a person's values appropriately balanced.

✳ One thing should be apparent: Life pulsates with so many pregnant potentialities for good that it should not be wasted.

✳ In the existential confrontation with death one discovers that the only thing that really matters is *life*. We should do all that we can to perpetuate, fulfill, and enhance it. Every moment of each day counts. Our best recourse is to live life with intensity and exhilaration—in thought, experience, action, and deed.

✳ *My* life, taken in toto, is *my* project; it is *my* own work of art. Every part of my life fits together; its every pattern, color, tone, lustre, and fabric is of my own making.

* Yet dying is part of the spectacle of living. One should face it bravely.

* We have nothing to fear of death—if there is no pain—since there is no guarantee of an afterlife. We will no doubt feel remorse and sorrow in leaving such an exciting world—particularly if our death is premature.

* To withhold the reality of an impending death, or to not permit a dying person to confront it if he or she so wishes, can be an indignity against the human spirit. To be forced to die in a hospital, to be condemned to spend one's last hours and days alone in impersonal surroundings may be cruel and unnecessary punishment. A person should be allowed, if he or she so desires, to pass away in comfortable surroundings with cherished relatives and friends in sight, to have one last glimpse of the beautiful world.

❋ No doubt one will have regrets in dying about the things that one did or did not do, those who may have been hurt, egregious mistakes and blunders one may have made. But one can also have fond remembrances of things past—memories of love, affection, friendship, creative activity, achievement, exhilaration, joy, and exuberance.

❋ With tears in one's eyes a person will part company, perhaps even with fists clenched. But if a person has lived fully, bursting at the seams, finally, when there is no energy or vitality left, hopefully one can say to others in departing, "How marvelous it has been, and how sad that you have not found the key." Some happiness is within everyone's grasp. Life, no matter how long, is too short; yet one can bear death with courage and pathos. And perhaps, if a person is fortunate, he can say: "I loved life, and I did not waste it. It was wonderful while it lasted!"

For a New Future

*I*t is time that we turn away from the ancient dogmas and doctrines of the past, and reach out to a new future. Using science, reason, and free inquiry blended with empathy and caring, it is possible to build a new civilization not mired in the false illusions spawned in the infancy of the race. This points to a new global culture to which the common moral decencies, ethical excellences, exuberance, and eupraxsophy can contribute. Planetary Humanism can help humankind achieve a new stage of human development.